Daily
AFFIMATIONS

365 Positive Affirmations To Attract Health, Wealth, Abundance, Happiness And Success Every Day!

- Author -

Rebecca Hunter

Codice ISBN: 9781689635387

Disclaimer

This book has been written for information purposes only. Every effort has been made to make this book as complete and accurate as possible. However, there may be mistakes in typography or content. Also, this book provides information only up to the publishing date. Therefore, this book should be used as a guide - not as the ultimate source.

The purpose of this book is to educate. The author and the publisher do not warrant that the information contained in this book is fully complete and shall not be responsible for any errors or omissions. The author and publisher shall have neither liability nor responsibility to any person or entity with respect to any loss or damage caused or alleged to be caused directly or indirectly by this book.

TABLE OF CONTENT

INTRODUCTION

I n his famous novel, The Strangest Secret, Earl Nightingale said, you're what you believe. He considered that when a individual simply feeds his head with negative thoughts, he'll encounter life through a dark lens.

Little things which shouldn't impact him will finally become larger than they actually are because their head is centered on the worst potential result instead of the very best. He spoke about the way the man who resides with largely negative ideas will concentrate his thoughts on all of his problems in contrast to the opportunities .

Regrettably, many people now, live with this type of mindset. With the 24/7 accessibility to media outlets around the world, it is no wonder , and much more folks are not able to accomplish a blissful and optimistic frame of mind. Today's media understands that "negative news sells," that supplies them with all the rationale to engage in fear mongering. Regrettably, it functions. This is only because we're intended to endure, rather than flourish. When it did, there could be many more people flourishing both personally and financially.

Luckily, our heads are amazingly effective and therefore are capable of exceptionally awesome things. That is where positive slogans get involved.

Understanding Affirmations and How They Work

Affirmations are hints and ideas that you give to yourself and could be either negative or positive. Since you give yourself those hints, you're feeding them in your subconscious mind, and that's what finally can help to ascertain your emotional attitude.

Should you nourish positive ideas and ideas to your subconscious mind, this may finally develop a positive or positive psychological attitude, and if you feed your mind with great, and happy thoughts, your mind starts to take these ideas as reality as your subconscious is not able to distinguish between your creativity and your own reality.

Once you always inject positive thoughts into your subconscious mind, it is going to begin to trust them as being the fact, and it begins to function generating comparable thought patterns.

As soon as your ideas become favorable, you begin to be optimistic about your own life and the world around you. Your ideas, after all, build you. By thinking positively, you can empower yourself and develop a wholesome mindset and a wholesome frame of mind that's always thinking of expansion, advancement, and fresh thoughts. When you produce a positive idea in mind, it goes out and begins drawing towards you useful and constructive opportunities which could help you meet your objectives.

Here is the way positive affirmations operate, and using them every day will slowly turn into a mutually favorable person mindset.

Why You Should Use Affirmations

Emile Coule has been a renowned psychologist that you popularized the custom of positive affirmations by giving the world with a strong, powerful tool to assist individuals from all jobs caked success and prosperity. Afterward, various medical and scientific studies are conducted to demonstrate the potency of the advantages obtained with daily exercise. These studies have shown that affirmations are really incredibly beneficial and will help dramatically alter your life for the better.

Their counterparts that did not use affirmations daily. She considers that affirmations can help significantly boost your self-esteem, leading to enhanced performance in various facets of life.

Affirmations help to construct a constructive and feel-good mindset.

Whenever you've got a positive mindset, you typically believe favorably a vast majority of this time, along with your optimistic mindset can readily be utilized to combat negative ideas which may attempt to infiltrate your mind. This helps to construct self-belief, which then shapes your self-confidence instilling the 'I will' mindset. When you begin taking actions, you finally take control of your targets and achieve success in life.

The use of affirmations to be successful in each pillar of your daily life mostly depends upon a few requirements.

How to Generate Affirmations Work For You

Compounds are the way the brain communicates with the human own body. The compound relations are made for every one of those experiences on your life. When you replicate activities often, it is helpful to fortify these neural links. It's a continuous reorganization process on mind each time you do it.

Your activities do not just need to be physical, but may also be psychological and include your own ideas in addition to your own words. The more you believe, do or talk something the more powerful the more neural pathways become.

The question we face is that most your over 60,000 ideas that cross your mind every day are unfavorable, due to our survival and biological instincts to continue to beliefs, customs, and experiences which were bad. But when you decide to believe positively, you are able to change your subconscious mind to violate this inclination to fill your mind with negative ideas and begin focusing more on the positive things in your lifetime.

The majority of the ability of emotion and thought exists inside you. It follows that you already understand how to feel joyful, joyful, adored, etc.. On the other hand, the matter often lies within the ideas that you continue to strengthen as you abide by a negative storyline. You tell yourself that you're poor, unloved, unhappy, but wish to be happy, loved, and great. To create affirmations work for you, it's vital that you make a concerted effort to modify your self-talk so you are able to fortify the feelings and feelings you have inside that you wish to bring into the forefront of your lifetime. If you change your ideas into the present tense, it generates control within the pathways on the mind. Additionally, it opens doors for one to accomplish incredible things.

Scientific studies have shown again and again that embracing positive affirmations on your life can produce strong modifications to your psyche. The daily exercise of positive affirmations has been associated with improved academic performance, better athletic performance, lower anxiety levels, better functionality when handling challenging activities, and making healthy lifestyle decisions. Regardless of how or why you're searching to practice positive affirmations, there's evidence out there that it functions nicely.

The custom of integrating positive affirmation into your everyday life is a private process and can be something which you have to develop if you'd like them to function for your lifetime. This usually means you could decide on a positive affirmation that fits on your own life, but you are also able to tweak it and alter it so it works best for the situation. If you're still struggling with the procedure, you can try the next steps.

1. Maintain a diary with you constantly, and write your thoughts. The procedure for writing helps you to incorporate the ideas more completely to your subconscious mind, much quicker than if you were to sort them out. Writing them down makes them intentional.

2. Each time you see that you're thinking about something negative about yourself or your life, write it down in your diary.

3. Below or alongside the negative idea, rewrite it into Something positive which negates the message. Be certain you write it in the present tense and contain the announcement, "I'm."

4. Want to replicate it.

This Procedure is meant to assist you to identify the negative Comment on mind and shed light on the occasions when These negative ideas look. If You've Got the time to document the Time and day and a tiny bit about the scenario that's resulting in Negative ideas, you can start to recognize patterns in your Ideas and activities. These "triggers" may Wind up resulting in Negative results, or you'll be able to rewrite the link to Something which contributes to a favorable outcome.

If you unveil your ideas to positive affirmations, you would like to make certain to make it something you will actually recall. It should immediately address the issue but you need to be brief and easy.

It may also be immensely beneficial to integrate creative visualization to the procedure. If you do not understand what creative visualization is, it's a meditative thought process that permits you to establish your heartfelt desires, by simply thinking about them. Employing creative visualization with your positive affirmations has a vital role in bringing what you need. With creative visualization, you may make a more loving and optimistic picture of yourself.

If you integrate creative visualization in your confirmation practice, you have to take action to unwind and get to a calm, meditative frame of mind. As soon as you are able to enter a state of complete relaxation, you can start to sketch out the psychological particulars about what it is you're attempting to manifest in your lifetime. By way of instance, you do not only need to consider getting a new vehicle, but you want to consider your driving at the true vehicle that you want. For the creative visualization process to operate, you need to think it will occur, like when you're reciting your positive affirmations.

Exercise will create your affirmations better. You do not have to try for perfection, but instead you need to target for a positive encounter. Should you would like to change your mindset and your existing position in life and begin to live the life which you want, positive affirmations can be a remarkably powerful tool that will assist you get there.

3 Errors to Avoid On Your Daily Affirmation Practice

Thousands of individuals use positive affirmations to acquire success and realize their own dreams. But, you can find equally as many who exercise affirmations but not see results. This is because they aren't using them properly.

Listed below are 3 errors that you would like to prevent in your everyday affirmation practice if you'd like them to work for you.

1. Giving Up Too Early

As soon as you begin with your clinic, the repeat has a lasting impact which will continue to build on itself. Additionally, each time you say the announcement you considerably magnify the outcomes. The error that lots of men and women make is they give up the procedure entirely too early. If you give up too soon, you do not offer the affirmations time to put into your own subconscious.

2. Using a Different Affirmation Every Day

Working with a different affirmation daily is like attempting to operate on a dozen different projects at the same time. Since every job requires your power and focus, you can not help but change your attention and attempt from project to project. But if you would like to see results straight away, then you need to concentrate on just 1 affirmation and stay with it. If it has to do with affirmations, it's about focus. To create your affirmations powerful, you've got to use exactly the identical confirmation daily for a minimum of 30 days.

3. Lack of Attention Mastery

If you have been utilizing positive affirmations for a while and have yet to attain outcomes, and you have tried everything else, then it might indicate that you are not completely focusing your attention about the affirmation. The truth is that most people have very brief attention spans, and they're distracted continuously for example toddlers. By minding your positive affirmations every day, you can discover how to learn your focus. Once you're able to find out to master your focus, you will begin to master your own reflections.

5 Powerful Strategies for Using Affirmations to Get What You Want

1. They May Be Used Anywhere

The very best thing about affirmations is that you can use them everywhere and at any time. For example, if you are heading into an interview for a new job, you may use a simple affirmation to assist you to calm your nerves.

2. Keep Them Short

You need to be certain you keep your affirmations easy, brief, and to the point. Your statements will be more effective when they are quick, one-liners which you can repeat to yourself over and over again. Keeping them brief will also help you remember them so that you can repeat them anywhere.

3. Maintain Them Favorable

Our subconscious minds can't differentiate between a positive and negative affirmation and will take on either one. Should you say yourself, "I'm not going to fail this test", it will only here, going to fail this test. To keep your affirmations positive, you should instead say, "I am passing this test".

4. Repeat Them Every Morning

Start to repeat your affirmations daily to help encourage your goals daily. When you wake up in the morning, look over your schedule and come up with the best affirmation that will support the accomplishment of the aims for the day. After some time, you may find some common positive affirmations that work best for you frequently.

5. Record Them in Your Voice

Just take the opportunity to make a recording of you repeating your affirmations. You can then listen to the tapes on your way to work or as needed. Consider adding some soothing music into the background to make them more useful.

In case you haven't had success with your daily affirmations, don't stress, you just have to make a couple of straightforward adjustments to your daily practice. Steer clear of the errors listed above and keep these five tips in mind when you are using your affirmations, and you'll achieve everything you need quickly.

Chapter 1: Affirmations for Attracting Health

I t's entirely too easy to take our health for granted nowadays. A cookie cutter here, a candy bar there. In the beginning, nothing happens, but slowly, over time our weight starts to creep upward, and we start to feel exhausted and down in the dumps. And of course all the negative emotions that come along with it: anger, stress, and frustration along with a drop in our self-esteem.

Luckily, becoming healthier is relatively straightforward. All it takes is making a choice to make a change in our lives. This applies to both our mental and physical well-being. Consciously making small, apparently trivial, but positive choices every day will deliver results that are often surprising. After three weeks we develop a habit and unexpectedly discover that it is not only become easier, but automatic to make better healthier choices.

Just like with our bodily wellbeing, you can reinforce your mind by nourishing it with developing your skills and talents, good books, spending additional time with friends, and seeking out more adventures that offer us opportunities for growth. Here are some tips for maintaining and enhancing your health.

1. I'm filled with power and life.

2. I'm in charge of my condition in any way times.

3. I'm happy and always have control over the way I feel.

4. I prefer to be filled with gratitude and joy.

5. I'm more than I appear to be, and in my are the Forces of this Universe.

6. My motive for eating wholesome foods would be to fuel my body.

7. Becoming healthy is far better than every other flavor on the planet.

8. My wholesome body is produced by my thoughts that are healthy.

9. My body is my temple.

10. I'm worthy of becoming healthy.

11. My Everyday customs are helping me to become fitter and happier.

12. I decide to eat healthy since the food I consume is a building material for my entire body.

13. I eat healthy foods that give energy.

14. I can eat for pleasure or societal reasons so long as I do it Responsibly and remain in my rules that I put beforehand.

15. I get loads of energizing and relaxed sleep.

16. I make healthy decisions and respect the human anatomy I have been given.

17. The water I drink cleanses my entire body and provides me the Clarity of thoughts I want to be successful.

18. I really like how it seems to be wholesome.

19. I feel a profound sense of well-being.

20. My body heals quickly and easily.

21. I take a considerable quantity of time to clean my thoughts.

22. I spend on the health of my own body and mind.

23. My heart is strong and healthy.

24. My fitness and wellness are a priority.

25. I have ample power to live my entire life.

26. Living a wholesome lifestyle is important to me.

27. I like my body. It takes me anywhere.

28. My body develops fitter and stronger daily.

29. I must be healthy.

30. I'm in charge of my health.

31. I'm great, and that I radiate an abundance of pleasure and gratitude.

32. I respect my entire body, and I'm surrounded by other people who desire Me to become healthy.

33. I trust that the signs my body sends to me

personally.

34. I feel great, my entire body feels great, and that I radiate nothing but Superior feelings.

35. I'm in possession of a healthy body and a healthy mind.

36. I'm vigorous and lively.

37. I let go of all bad feelings in my about the others, events, And everything. I forgive everyone who's connected with me.

38. My entire body is healthy, I'm rich, and my thoughts are sensible.

39. I'm looking forward to a healthy future since I take care Of my body today.

40. I'm grateful for my body.

41. Peace flows throughout my body, mind, and soul.

42. I like my life.

43. I'm worthy of very good health.

44. I care for my own body with real empathy.

45. I'm doing everything in my power to maintain my body healthy.

46. I have a powerful and powerful immune system. I'm able to Treat germs, viruses, and germs.

47. My body is totally free of pain.

48. My body heals itself, and I feel better each day.

49. I keep my own bodyweight fast and easily daily.

50. I'm fully in control of my health, health, and Healing.

51. I love and love my body, mind, and soul.

52. My skin is clean, luminous, and glowing.

53. I'm capable of being in a position to keep my

ideal weight.

54. I'm a powerful, healthy, healthy, and energetic individual who is capable of handling whatever arises.

55. I'll devote 20-30 minutes per day.

56. I'm enthusiastic, lively, and energetic every second.

57. I like eating balanced, healthy, and wholesome meals.

58. I have the entire capability to restrain my health and exercise center.

59. I really like to eat wholesome meals and exercise every day.

60. I'm the receiver of a lively mind, body, and soul and soul Luminous health.

61. I like my everyday workout regimen.

62. I'm healthy, fit, and healthy, and participate in regular physical fitness.

63. Each day that I get closer and closer to my own ideal weight.

64. I eat healthy nutritious, energy-giving and balanced meals That advantage my whole body.

65. My body makes fitter, stronger, and much more lively with each passing day.

66. My entire body is a temple. It's sacred, clean, and full of a feeling of goodness.

67. I breathe fine and profoundly, exercise frequently, and nourish my Body healthy, healthy foods.

68. My everyday thoughts support my entire body to become fitter.

69. I give my body what it requires.

70. I feel good, and my entire body heals quickly.

71. I fill my mind with positive ideas.

72. I use my own body in a way that produces

positive emotions.

73. I often smile and stand upright.

74. I release the past and enjoy the current moment.

75. I relax my jaw and maintain my teeth split slightly.

76. I relax my body frequently and let my body rest once it should.

77. I really do things that are good for the body.

78. I'm unbelievably healthy, and I really like it.

79. I'm powerful and feel great about myself and how healthy am.

80. I'm at peace with my wellbeing.

81. My head is brilliant, and my spirit is tranquil.

82. I sleep in peace and wake up with amazing joy.

83. I enjoy exercising every day and filling my

body with healthy foods.

84. I'm fit, lively, healthy and attractive.

85. I'm stunning both indoors and outside.

86. I Take Care of myself by exercising, eating right, and getting enough sleep.

87. I love, care for, and nurture my entire body, and it cares for me.

88. I'm extremely beautiful, fit and attractive.

89. I'm completely relaxed and full of all the peace of mind and serenity.

90. I produce healing energy during my entire life.

91. I am capable of demonstrating maximum strength and wellness.

Chapter 2 - Affirmations for Attracting Wealth

A smart person once said, money is not everything, but it's up there with oxygen. From the way you bring it, make it, spend it, save it, and invest it. In case you've got a negative relationship with cash, you can discover that your fiscal situation is in a continuous state of disarray.

Whether or not you encounter negative or positive feelings about cash, there's not any denying the significant role it plays in our own lives and the lives of those near us. If you're now experiencing money blocks, you may use these affirmations that will assist you build a wealth mindset. As you browse the affirmations, consider how getting more money on your life will impact you.

Money will come to those men and women that have a wealth mindset. The gratitude and prosperity affirmations must lift your imperceptible money magnet so you can begin bringing plenty of riches in your life.

92. Wealth pours in my life every day.

93. My bank accounts grows every day.

94. I've attained financial security in my entire life.

95. I'm full of gratitude and pleasure, and I

adore that an increasing number of money is flowing into me every day.

96. Cash is flowing to me personally in avalanches of wealth from surprising sources.

97. I must be wealthy and to get plenty of cash in my bank accounts.

98. All of my dreams, goals, and needs are instantly fulfilled.

99. The Universe is really on my side, and it's directing me toward riches and abundance.

100. I really like money and all it can purchase.

101. I'm thankful that my net worth increases considerably every year.

102. Suggestions on how to earn more money come to me frequently.

103. I'm great about cash.

104. I will do great things with the money I've.

105. I discharge all of my negative thoughts about money and permit monetary prosperity to enter my entire life.

106. Opportunities to make more money come to me effortlessly.

107. I attract money easily and I now have more wealth than I ever thought possible.

108. I'm wealthy, and that I feel incredibly great about it.

109. I have a fantastic relationship with money.

110. I'm grateful for all of the cash I have in my bank accounts.

111. Every day I'm attracting more cash into my own life.

112. I attract money effortlessly.

113. I'm a money magnet, and cash will always be drawn to me.

114. I am not lounging into greater prosperity.

115. I release all resistance to cash.

116. I deserve to get a whole lot of money in my bank accounts.

117. Suggestions for making money are openly entering my entire life.

118. Abundance is about me, and that I sense gracious about it.

119. Becoming wealthy is my normal state of becoming.

120. The Universe is assisting me draw cash into my life .

121. I'm booming, and I am thankful for all of the great things in my life.

122. It's extremely simple for me to earn more cash.

123. I'm a natural-born money maker.

124. I'm ready and prepared to get more cash today.

125. My earnings considerably raises each year.

126. Earning cash is simple for me.

127. Success is my birthright

128. Thank you, Universe for letting me reside in prosperity.

129. I am the founder of my own life.

130. I've always been destined to become rich.

131. I find a whole lot of chances in my personal own life to make prosperity and prosperity.

132. I'm thankful I get to stay in prosperity.

133. I live in prosperity.

134. Money comes to me effortlessly.

135. I see unlimited opportunities for creating more wealth in my entire life.

136. I'm thankful for the cash that I have.

137. Getting wealthy and with a good deal of

cash affords me the chance to make the planet a better location.

138. It seems fantastic to have plenty of cash.

139. The Universe responds to my wealth mindset by giving me more chances to generate income easily.

140. I imagine being wealthy each and every single day, and I'm out good vibrations to the Universe regarding cash.

141. I am a cash magnet that brings money from all sorts of places.

142. I'm abundant daily, in every single way.

143. I'm gracious for all the wealth I get daily.

144. My money multiplies since I pay for myself.

145. I always am in a position to discover and develop more ways to earn money easily.

146. Money is a significant part of my entire life, and I give it the time and care it deserves.

147. Cash permits me to assist more individuals.

148. Cash enables me to spend more time with my nearest and dearest.

149. Money enables me to have wonderful adventures.

150. Having more cash is a great thing for my entire life and enables me to do what I need.

151. I really like money and all the things which let me achieve it.

152. I deserve to be wealthy and to live my life in prosperity.

153. I always have a significant excess of cash in the close of each month.

154. I always learn from other people who reside in fiscal abundance.

155. My activities create a great deal of value for many others.

156. I'm a man of amazing price.

157. I make my money work for me.

158. I'm a fantastic money manager.

159. I'm thankful for the ability that the Universe gives me to earn a great deal of cash.

160. My fiscal reality is within my overall control.

161. Cash is my slave.

162. I have all I want to make financial abundance in my entire life.

163. There's sufficient money for me to make a rewarding life.

164. I hope that the Universe will always satisfy your own requirements.

165. I'm great at handling my money. I'm the master of my cash, and I'm in charge of my finances.

166. I'm a millionaire. I think like a millionaire, I behave like a millionaire, and that I feel like a millionaire.

167. I let wealth to input my entire life. I let prosperity to input my entire life. I allow abundance to input my entire life.

168. I'm fully receptive to all of the riches which life offers me.

169. My achievement is important and essential.

170. All my dreams have come true.

171. I create riches; hence I'm always wealthy.

172. I hope to attain success in all my endeavors and permit achievement to be my normal condition in life.

173. I am in a position to proceed back mistakes and challenges quickly and easily.

174. Cash comes to me within a simple and effortless manner.

175. I align myself with all the energy of riches and prosperity.

176. I use my cash to enhance my life and the lives of those near me.

177. Money produces a beneficial effect on my own life.

178. I let my prosperity to enlarge, and I reside in comfort and pleasure daily.

179. I am in a position to earn a lot of money doing exactly what I love, and I am completely supported in all of my ventures.

180. I think positive cash thoughts every day.

181. I've lots of cash for my requirements and lots for the demands of the others.

182. By living my goal, I bring abundance in my entire life.

Chapter 3 – Affirmations for Attracting Happiness

Happiness is a state of contentment and well-being. The very first step that you will need to take to become happy is to change your ideas. Affirmations are a terrific tool for this since they can help replace the limiting beliefs that you hold with much more empowering ones. It's essential to be aware that you don't wish to attempt and induce the negative ideas to evaporate, but instead you want to understand to become conscious of the ideas and accept them without even placing some judgment on these. By being present and mindful, you will begin to discover the negative ideas will gradually start to fade in the background.

A lot of people around the globe are searching for happiness in large events or things, when actually there's frequently more energy in bringing happiness from common experiences. You do not wish to wait to be pleased, particularly in the event that it's possible to decide to be happy here and now. Additionally, it's essential to consider that your structure is a remarkably important piece for feeling joyful. You won't ever feel happy if you've got your head and a frown on your face.

When you lift up your head and put a grin on your face, you'll feel a good deal better, and it'll be easier to create a positive mindset. Don't forget to use your own body in a positive manner when you use these affirmations.

183. Each single day, and in every way, I am experiencing an increasing number of pleasure and pleasure in my entire life.

184. Happiness is my normal state of becoming.

185. I deserve to be happy.

186. By being happy each day, I will help other people to become happy in their own lives.

187. I'm thankful for all of the happy feelings that accompany me anywhere I go.

188. I spread joy to others and consume pleasure from others in return.

189. I am so happy and thankful for my life my perspective on life is remarkably positive.

190. Being joyful is simple for me.

191. I'm grateful for each and every moment of each day since I know it won't ever return.

192. My future is bright, and I am incredibly thankful for this.

193. I always think inspiring thoughts.

194. I'm very thankful for the air I am breathing, the water that I have access to, and the food in my fridge.

195. I'm thankful because I have what I want to live my entire life.

196. I begin daily in a state of immense happiness and joy.

197. I'm a happy giver and a happy receiver of great things in my own life.

198. The world is going to be a better location and more joyful place because I had been here.

199. I'm an unstoppable force permanently.

200. I trust myself as my internal wisdom understands reality.

201. I breathe in joy with each and every breath I take.

202. I wake up feeling thankful for this lifetime

and filled with pleasure.

203. I am so pleased and thankful because I expect to live the life span of my fantasies.

204. I'm always learning and improving new things which make me happy.

205. I'm present and feel tremendous pleasure at this instant.

206. I am able to change any negative into a positive, regardless of what it really is.

207. I'm a very positive person who has amazing gifts to share with the entire world.

208. I am the founder of the own life, my months, my weeks, along with my years and I opted to make joy and happiness.

209. I choose to make my own life a masterpiece worth recalling.

210. I'm alive, and the world around me seems fresh and new.

211. Life is fantastic, and I really like living.

212. You will find infinite opportunities for me to experience pleasure and happiness daily.

213. I change any barrier into abundant chances.

214. I'm forever grateful for the abundance in my entire life.

215. I'm open to accepting new journeys and starts in my own life. I'm always learning, expanding, and unlocking fresh and promising chances.

216. Every moment I love the completeness of my trip and I am conscious that by enjoying the completeness of my trip a realize greater joy, peace, and pleasure.

217. The little joys in life include great happiness for my days once I become more aware of the presence.

218. I admire everything and everybody around

me, and that I perform even small actions with a great deal of pleasure, love, and love.

219. I'm powerful, creative, and joyful, and that I use my own mistakes as stepping stone to develop to some wiser person.

220. I appreciate internal peace and recognize that being is totally okay. I reside with my fact, and my joy is as much inside me as it's me outside.

221. I'm really thankful to the Universe with this glorious and fantastic life. I'm really blessed and thankful to everyone who has touched my life, and it has made it worthwhile living.

222. Happy ideas and circumstances are attracted to me obviously. I'm always landing in happy conditions.

223. I'm happy doing random acts of kindness, love, compassion, love, and enjoyment. My love contributes to more joy and love in penetrating my life.

224. I'm loving, joyful, and sort.

225. I am really thankful and appreciative of what that I have, such as love, joy and empathy for others.

226. I really feel a complete sense of happiness, love, and enjoyment right now and exude this energy through the day.

227. I feel stunning inside and outside while setting my own sense of beauty through favorable energy, rich love, and joy.

228. My prosperity of love, joy, and positive strength lets me step in the day and achieve everything I put my head in.

229. I allow myself to go through the goodness that surrounds me and keep positive energy that flows through the afternoon to nourish my body, mind, and soul.

230. I opt to pull pleasure for my life, and that I deserve to be genuinely happy and joyful at what I set out to perform.

231. Now is your day for a new start, and that I welcome the afternoon with refreshed eyes and a mind-boggling mind.

232. Abundance is flowing through my entire day, and that I have all of the love, joy, enthusiasm, imagination, and vitality to create my day special.

233. Each moment that I'm living, I become happier and happier with my life.

234. Every cell in my body is pulsating with joy, joy, positivity, and prosperity.

235. I'm happier now than I've ever been.

236. Happiness is something which is contagious. I know this, and I work to spread joy around to other people, which brings joy back to me tenfold.

237. My pleasure aids the people in my life feel more joyful.

238. My joyful attitude brings other happiness in

my life.

239. I'm immensely thankful for my superb life. I'm grateful to everybody who's made me happy and that has made my life worth living.

240. I'm happy when I make progress toward attaining my objectives.

241. I concentrate more on my current happiness compared to errors from my own past.

242. I am able to pick myself up and lift my own spirits.

243. I feel a huge sense of joy and peace in myself.

244. I'm a positive person and also select to get a positive outlook on life.

245. I am prepared to handle whatever comes my way along with joy and a positive mindset.

246. I'm happy; I'm healthy; I'm powerful.

247. Each single morning I wake up feeling happy in my life and my future.

248. I approach everything in my life with a sense of humor and like to laugh along with other people.

249. While I think of happy thoughts, my entire life brightens and lightens.

250. Being joyful is a high priority in my entire life, and that I recall to exercise this feeling daily.

251. I let myself to completely enjoy the small moments that I see around me daily.

252. I'm always searching for more ways to attract joy and laughter into my life.

253. I'm always able to discover a reason to smile daily.

254. I'm completely delighted with the choices that I create in my entire life.

255. I'm always friendly with different people

and grin at them.

256. I spread pleasure anywhere I go.

257. I dedicate myself to create the greatest possible degree of pleasure in my own life.

258. My life is continually overflowing with joy and happiness.

259. I operate joyfully toward most of my goals and dreams.

260. I'm always happy because I'm doing good things with my life.

261. I'm worthy of love and enjoyment.

262. I welcome joy and pleasure in my life.

263. I'm happy because I live my life completely daily.

264. I rest in full bliss and enjoyment whenever I go to sleep since I know what's fine in my own Universe.

265. I'm the happiest and content person in this world.

266. I'm glad that happiness originates from inside me and that I live every second to the fullest.

267. The chances which life presents me are infinite.

268. I float happily and at a content fashion in my entire own world.

269. I decide to live a joyful, serene, and balanced lifestyle.

270. I find joy, joy, and delight in the smallest of items.

271. I am able to tap into my innerspring of pleasure anytime I need and let a stream of pleasure, joy, and well-being.

272. I look at and watch the world around me with a grin because I can not help but feel all of the pleasure around me.

273. My pleasure succeeds and expands daily.

274. Each day that I wake up with a joyful grin on my face along with a feeling of enormous gratitude in my heart for all of the terrific moments that await me through the day.

Chapter 4 - Affirmations for Attracting Success

Everybody dreams of living a prosperous life, but not many men and women are fortunate enough to achieve that, even by their own estimations. At the society level, power and wealth are recognized as the typical indicators of true achievement, and it's not difficult to see why. This is as it isn't hard to keep score or cash and it has a tendency to result from the visual presentation of what you can purchase with cash.

While each of the above is important that you think about, you are able to experience success for yourself on a daily basis. From the tiny daily activities that you take towards achieving significant objectives. While they might look as they are modest, these aims are the things where your long-term fantasies are created. It's necessary to observe the tiny things in your lifetime.

Repeating these tips for success on a daily basis can enable you to get to a prosperous mindset. A thriving mindset is one which includes positive and empowering beliefs about achievement in all parts of your own life. It's been stated before that people today fear success more than failure, and with that sort of mindset, it's tough to attain anything outstanding in life. The next affirmations can allow you to conquer any psychological blocks which may be holding you back from your dreams.

275. I'm proud of everything I've achieved in my entire life.

276. I have the capacity and ability to make all of the success and prosperity that I want in my entire life.

277. My mind is totally free of immunity and can be open to all of the new and exciting possibilities .

278. I deserve to be more prosperous, and I am worthy of getting all of the good that life has to give me.

279. I'm grateful for all of the skills and abilities that lead to my everyday success.

280. The Universe is full of unlimited possibilities and chances for me to really have a profession I love.

281. I'm open-minded and excited in regards to fully explore new paths and possibilities for achievement in my entire life.

282. I understand every chance that knocks on my door and I seize it instantly.

283. Each day I find exciting, promising, and intriguing new avenues to travel.

284. I see and experience prosperity anywhere I look.

285. I really like my job. It's satisfying, gratifying and part of my journey toward greater achievement.

286. My dream is in excellent harmony with my private and professional worth.

287. I work with enthusiastic, inspiring and interesting men and women who share my zest for work and achievement.

288. By generating success for me personally, I'm also creating a wealth of chances for the achievement of the others.

289. I'm confident, strong and calm as I take on fresh challenges.

290. I attract strong and successful men and women who know, motivate, and inspire me every day.

291. I observe each goal I reach with thankfulness, joy, and happiness.

292. The more successful I become, the more strong and positive I believe in the remainder of my life.

293. I'll forever pull in the ideal situation in the best time in my entire life. I'm always in the ideal place at the ideal moment.

294. I'm thankful for all of the success that's continually flowing into my own life.

295. I completely trust my intuition to guide me making wise and smart decisions in my personal life.

296. I keep myself focused on my vision and pursue my regular work with zeal and enthusiasm.

297. Each day is full of plenty of fresh possibilities, ideas, and paths which bring great inspiration into my life.

298. Success comes effortlessly and easily for me since I excel in all that I do.

299. I take absolute pride within my inborn ability to make worthy contributions.

300. I expect positive benefits in all I do, and consequently, I obviously attract me.

301. I'm blessed to pull strong and amazing mentors who kindly share their knowledge, understanding, and thoughts with me.

302. As I allow success and prosperity in my life, more, doors to success and opportunity open for me.

303. I set incredibly significant standards for

myself, and I am ready to always live up to these criteria.

304. I have an inexhaustible source of amazing new ideas that help me become a successful person with every passing day.

305. I'm always developing a lifetime of success, joy, and prosperity.

306. I genuinely love the individual that I'm, and that I always draw in people who respect and respect me for the exceptional individual I am.

307. By having an inspirational, positive, and highly effective effect on people around me, I'm making the world a better place for everybody to live.

308. I dream and think big, that constantly brings me achievement.

309. Every day I wake up and dress for success, prosperity, and prosperity in your body, mind, and soul.

310. I'm really grateful for the success I have achieved and the prosperity and fiscal prosperity I love daily.

311. I'm enthusiastic and passionate about becoming more effective in my entire life.

312. The Universe is constantly helping me achieve all of my targets and desires.

313. My fantasies constantly manifest right before my eyes.

314. The Universe's riches are always circulating throughout my entire life and bringing me avalanches of success and prosperity.

315. I'm driven, ambitious, motivated, and inspired by my life's goals every day.

316. I have the entire capability to lift my spirits up whenever I need.

317. I believe it is simple and simple to be optimistic daily.

318. Success is naturally and easily attracted to

me in every area of my own life.

319. My teachings for prosperity, achievement, and enjoyment constantly maintain positive results.

320. Other men and women are driven and motivated by my achievement.

321. I'm decisive in all of my activities that have contributed to greater achievement, prosperity, and joy in my entire life.

322. It's simple for me to accomplish all of my goals in life.

323. The Universe is my buddy, also it helps me achieve all of my fantasies, needs, and intentions easily.

324. Other men and women are drawn to me because I'm incredibly profitable.

325. I always work to improve all of the aspects of my life and am rewarded with victory.

326. I have the profound desire and willpower to

grow to great heights of success.

327. I wholeheartedly give myself into the Universe, and in return, it stinks me with boundless rewards and achievement.

328. The vision I've generates a triumph which surrounds me in my everyday life.

329. Accomplishing all of my aims is remarkably simple and simple for me.

330. My life is a remarkably amazing, beautiful, and enjoyable trip.

331. My thoughts and beliefs create my own reality, and I am the master of my ideas.

332. I possess the capacity to make my entire life in precisely the manner I desire.

333. Everything I want, desire, and desire is out there waiting for me to take it.

334. I'm filled with unlimited positive thoughts, positive energy, and positive activities daily.

335. I hope for greatness and success.

336. Today and every day I take a few steps toward fulfilling my targets and getting everything that I need.

337. My thoughts, tenacity, positive energy, and capability can move mountains and assist me attain my objectives.

338. I'm refreshed, driven, determined, and eager to excel now and each day.

339. My thoughts, ideas, and beliefs are seeds for my achievement.

340. I'm enough and will always be sufficient.

341. Now is a superb day, and that I have everything I want to make it good.

342. I'm making intelligent decisions for my entire life since I have the knowledge I want to achieve that.

343. I surround myself with individuals who greatly contribute to my own growth and achievement.

344. I'm focused daily about the goals I want to achieve to succeed.

345. I'm intuitive and understand what leadership is ideal for my achievement.

347. I'm equipped with the knowledge and skills I want to adopt and attain success.

348. I'm constantly receiving the unlimited opportunities delivered to me from the Universe to assist me experience achievement.

349. I'm free from all of the obstacles which are holding me back from being powerful.

350. I'm excited and constantly available to follow new avenues to accomplish success.

351. I'm developing and studying the regions in life that make me free, joyful and filled with purpose.

352. I am happy and grateful for each purpose I accomplish and observe every person with pride.

353. I'm thankful for my success and pleasure.

354. I'm experiencing things daily which are leading me toward victory.

355. I'm always creating with aid me to increase the opportunities presented to me every day.

356. I'm filled with excitement and energy which helps me attain my targets and succeed.

357. I'm showing others how to think in me and my personal achievement through my belief in myself.

358. I'm living my very best life through my real self.

359. I'm clear about my goal, and that I understand what I want to do to achieve my targets and attain success.

360. I'm embracing everything which comes to me by the Universe.

361. I am always moving toward attaining my goals via my ongoing deliberate actions.

362. I'm creating new, positive habits which serve my objectives.

363. I'm open to unlimited chances for achievement which are introduced to me from the Universe.

364. I'm building my entire life on a foundation I set, and I am filling it with all the material I select.

365. I'm contributing great thoughts to the Universe.

CONCLUSION

It is not simple to alter how you see specific regions of your own life or to dig right into complicated and at times dark places. Positive affirmations are a tool you could use daily to assist you to relax or energize, concentrate or forgo, join or discharge. Everything depends on what you want and in which you think you want to go. You need to trust your instincts, so remain true to your course and remain positive.

You'll be able to instruct your brain to re-write the story to your narrative. You could begin at any location and proceed in the path of your objectives. And, if at any given stage, you end up off the path you're supposed to go in, fix a brand new verification and get going where you want to go. Your activities will then direct you to reality, and that is the way you can create incredible things happen in your lifetime. Everything begins with your own thoughts.

Now you have learned how to create affirmations work on your own life and have loads of tips about the best way best to call for your own desires and aims to attest, it's time to select one and get started copying yourself. Whenever your mind considers it, your activities will probably live it. And if your actions reside your truth, consequently, reflects it. Every day you need to opt to keep moving ahead and being optimistic. You need to think in yourself and your incredible purpose if you would like to manifest all of your heart desires with the support of positive affirmations.

Manufactured by Amazon.ca
Bolton, ON